Start TO Finish
Second Series

FROM Pumpkin TO Pie

LISA OWINGS

LERNER PUBLICATIONS COMPANY · Minneapolis

Lerner Publications Company
A division of Lerner Publishing Group, Inc.
241 First Avenue North
Minneapolis, MN 55401 USA

For reading levels and more information, look up this title at www.lernerbooks.com.

Library of Congress Cataloging-in-Publication Data

Owings, Lisa, author.
    From pumpkin to pie / by Lisa Owings.
        pages   cm. — (Start to finish, second series)
    Includes index.
    ISBN 978–1–4677–6018–8 (lib. bdg. : alk. paper)
    ISBN 978–1–4677–6287–8 (eBook)
    1. Pumpkin—Processing—Juvenile literature.
    2. Pumpkin—Juvenile literature. I. Title. II. Series:
Start to finish (Minneapolis, Minn.). Second series.
SB347.O95 2015
664.80562—dc23   2014023480

Manufactured in the United States of America
1 – CG – 12/31/14

TABLE OF Contents

Pumpkin Pie is my favorite. How is it made?

First, gardeners plant pumpkin seeds.

Pumpkin pie starts with pumpkin seeds. Gardeners choose seeds that will grow into small, sweet pumpkins. They plant the seeds early in spring. They make sure to place the seeds far enough apart. Pumpkins need room to grow.

Then gardeners help the pumpkins grow.

Pumpkin plants grow best in rich soil and lots of sunlight. Gardeners water them often. Soon, leaves and **vines** cover the ground. In summer, golden flowers **bloom** along the vines. Each **pollinated** flower becomes a pumpkin.

Ripe pumpkins are harvested in fall.

Over time, the pumpkins grow larger, and their color changes from green to orange. Gardeners tap their pumpkins. If a pumpkin sounds hollow, it is ready to be cut from the vine.

Next, the pumpkin is prepared for baking.

In the kitchen, gardeners become bakers. They wash the pumpkin and cut it in half. Then they scoop out the seeds. The bakers cut the pumpkin into smaller pieces.

Bakers cook the pumpkin meat.

Then the pumpkin is baked in the oven or cooked on the stove. The pumpkin becomes soft and flavorful.

The pumpkin is mixed with other ingredients.

Bakers mash the cooked pumpkin. Then they mix it with eggs, spices, and other ingredients. It's starting to smell like pumpkin pie!

Bakers pour the mixture into a pie crust.

Some bakers buy pie crust from a store. Others make their own. They might pinch around the edges of the dough to give the crust a pretty **pattern**. Then they pour the pumpkin pie filling into the unbaked crust.

They bake the pie.

The pie is almost ready. Bakers make sure the oven is the right temperature. Then they bake the pie until the filling is firm.

Finally, the pie is done!

The hardest part is waiting for the pie to cool. Then it is ready to eat! Some people top their pumpkin pie with whipped cream, while others love it plain. Enjoy your dessert!

Glossary

bloom: to produce flowers

harvested: gathered for use

hollow: having an empty space inside

pattern: a repeated design often used to decorate something

pollinated: given pollen (a special dust made by plants) from another plant. When a plant is pollinated, it is able to produce seeds.

vines: long plant stems that grow along the ground or cling to fences and other objects

Further Information

Brown, Renata Fossen. *Gardening Lab for Kids*. Beverly, MA: Quarry Books, 2014. Your whole family can use this book as a guide to explore and experiment with gardening.

Nelson, Robin. *Pumpkins*. Minneapolis: Lerner Publications, 2009. Learn all the details of the pumpkin's life cycle in this book.

Price, Pam. *Cool Pies & Tarts: Easy Recipes for Kids to Bake*. Edina, MN: Abdo, 2010. Want to try a dessert other than pumpkin pie? Ask an adult to help you bake some of the delicious pies and tarts in this recipe book.

Pumpkin Carving
http://www.abcya.com/pumpkin_carving.htm
Pumpkins aren't just for pie. Practice carving your own pumpkin online with this fun activity. Then you can try growing your own pumpkins to make jack-o'-lanterns.

Pumpkin Facts for Kids
http://www.sciencekids.co.nz/sciencefacts/food/pumpkins.html
Check out this website for more cool facts about pumpkins.

Index

Photo Acknowledgments

The images in this book are used with the permission of:
© Viktar Malyshchyts/Shutterstock.com, p. 1; © gsk2014/Shutterstock.com, p. 3; © DibasUA/Shutterstock.com, p. 5; © Samantha Nundy/Alamy, p. 7; © iStockphoto.com/GomezDavid, p. 9; © homydesign/iStock/Thinkstock, p. 11; © iStockphoto.com/supermimicry, p. 13; © Collins/Alamy, p. 15; © Blend Images/Alamy, p. 17; © iStockphoto.com/YinYang, p. 19; © Ryan McVay/Photodisc/Getty Images, p. 21.

Front cover: © Paul Poplis/StockFood Creative/Getty Images.

Main body text set in Arta Std Book 20/26.
Typeface provided by International Typeface Corp.